BERKLEE PRESS

A GUIDE TO JAZZ IMPROVISATION

JOHN LAPORTA

Berklee Press

Director: Dave Kusek
Managing Editor: Debbie Cavalier
Marketing Manager: Ola Frank
Sr. Writer/Editor: Jonathan Feist

ISBN 0-634-00763-7

1140 Boylston Street
Boston, MA 02215-3693 USA
(617) 747-2146

Visit Berklee Press Online at
www.berkleepress.com

DISTRIBUTED BY

HAL•LEONARD®
CORPORATION
7777 W. BLUEMOUND RD. P.O. BOX 13819
MILWAUKEE, WISCONSIN 53213

Visit Hal Leonard Online at
www.halleonard.com

DEDICATION

This method is dedicated to my son, John Jr. who helped provide the key to solving this problem of learning to improvise.

John LaPorta

CONTENTS

LESSON 9

LESSON 10

LESSON 11

LESSON 12

INTRODUCTION

John LaPorta

In 1967, I gave an introductory clinic on improvisation to high school students in a small town close to Pittsburgh. Included in my presentation were the usual basics; major tonality, fundamental chords, and scales. An hour and a half had gone by, in which time I thought I had given the students a clear picture as to how to begin improvising. I asked for questions.

One brave student raised his hand and asked, "Yeah, but, how do you improvise?"

At that moment, I realized that there was a disconnect—a basic flaw in the common approach to teaching improvisation, where we teach theory first and then expect the students to be able to somehow miraculously use it in context. It should be the other way around. Students should experience improvising, and then later, learn theory as a way of understanding what they are already doing.

The next morning, while I was waiting for my flight back to Boston, I sketched out an entirely new approach, the essence of which I have been using ever since. By using the pentatonic scale—a simpler and more natural scale for making up melodies—students can avoid playing wrong scale tones against wrong chords, which is often the result when the theoretical approach is employed. It gets students creating right away, and teaches chord theory only after the feel of chords is already under their fingertips.

We published the first version of this method in 1968, and it has become something of a classic in circles where improvisation is taught. I use it myself, and have been making slight modifications over the years, refining and updating the musical examples, and reworking the presentation of certain elements so that they would be more like what actually happens in a blues performance.

Here's how it works. Twelve Lessons present workshops that teach techniques of improvisation, which are then used in actual arrangements. The accompanying recording helps simulate what it is like to play with other musicians. Better than this, of course, is to find some other players and practice the materials in this book together.

Students coming to *A Guide to Jazz Improvisation* should have basic technical proficiency with their instrument and familiarity with notation. Ranges are moderate, and if you prefer to take something down an octave, please do so. The goal is to learn improvisation. Developing facility on an instrument should be a separate undertaking.

A Guide to Jazz Improvisation is not intended to take the place of conventional instruction with a private teacher—nothing could ever replace that. It will help develop your skills as a creative, expressive improviser. Once you complete these lessons and are comfortable improvising, you may wish to look at some more theoretical approaches to improvisation. Berklee Press and other publishers have many excellent titles that will help expand your vocabulary and introduce you to other techniques. For now, the most important thing is to acquire the basic skills and the spirit of improvisation. Fifty years of teaching music has proven to me that this is a uniquely effective approach.

LESSON 1

 Tuning note: B♭ Concert

THEORY

G Pentatonic Scale (five-note scale starting on G)

Legato-Staccato (smooth attack)

The note is attacked but not cut off. The attack of the succeeding note cuts off the current note.
The articulated vowel sound for this would be "doo-doo."

Study in Legato-Staccato

Swinging Eighth Notes

Eighth notes are often played as triplets.

Workshop 1

Write and play eight- and twelve-measure melodies using the G pentatonic scale, legato-staccato articulation, and swinging eighth notes.

Workshop 2

1. Practice legato-staccato articulations on major scales, chromatic scales, and any other music selections of your choice.

2. Write and play at least two original (eight-measure) melodies. Use the pentatonic scale and refer to the exercises below as guides.

Five Note Scale Exercise 1

Five Note Scale Exercise 2

2 RHYTHM TRAINING

Listen to CD Track 2.

1. Echo. Repeat each rhythm pattern you hear exactly as it sounds on the recording.

Recorded rhythm

You play (echo)

2. Answer. Answer each rhythm pattern you hear with your own improvised rhythm.

Recorded rhythm

You play (improvised answer)

Note: The figure above is a suggested illustration. You may play any rhythmic idea you wish.

For the two-measure rhythm patterns below:

1. **Memorize.** Practice each pattern until you can play it without looking at the music.

2. **Compose.** Write at least four of your own rhythm patterns. Play and memorize these as well.

3. **Improvise/Transcribe.** Invent at least four of your own patterns by ear, memorize them, and then write them down.

Challenge

With another player, try the following:

1. **Reading call-and-response.** Player 1 plays one of the above patterns. Player 2 repeats it without looking at the music. Then switch roles.

2. **Improvising call-and-response.** Player 1 improvises a two-measure rhythm pattern. Player 2 repeats it. Then switch roles.

PERFORMANCE EAR TRAINING

 Listen to CD Track 3.

1. **Echo.** Repeat each motive you hear exactly as it sounds on the recording.

Recorded melody

You play (echo)

2. Answer. Answer each motive you hear with your own improvised motive. Try to use varied rhythms and combinations of notes.

Recorded melody

You play (improvised answer)

Note: The melodic idea written above is a suggested illustration. You may play any melodic idea you wish. Your melodies should be derived from combinations of notes taken from the G pentatonic scale.

For the two-measure melodic motives below:

1. Memorize. Practice each motive until you can play it without looking at the music.

2. Compose. Write at least four of your own melodic motives. Play and memorize these as well.

3. Improvise/Transcribe. Invent at least four of your own motives by ear, memorize them, and then write them down.

Challenge

With another player, try the following:

1. Reading call-and-response. Player 1 plays one of the above motives. Player 2 repeats it without looking at the music. Then switch roles.

2. Improvising call-and-response. Player 1 improvises a two-measure motive. Player 2 repeats it. Then switch roles.

4

4 PERFORMANCE

1. Learn the melody as written.

2. Play along with the recording. Try to capture the same manner of phrasing and style of playing.

   A Section. Head. Full ensemble.
   - Melody for 16 measures (2 choruses)

   B Section. You solo.
   - 16 measures
   - Use combinations of notes derived from the G pentatonic scale to create your solo.

   C Section. Recorded solo.
   - 8 measures

   D Section. You solo.
   - 8 measures
   - Use the G pentatonic scale.
   - At *D.C. al Fine,* return to letter A.

   A Section (repeat). Head.
   - Melody for 7 measures

Note: When taking a D.C. al fine, a repeated section is only played once unless directed otherwise. *D.C.* (Da Capo) means go back to the beginning. *Fine* indicates the final ending.

Slash marks (////) mean "improvise here." One / lasts for one beat.

Backgrounds for "Origin"

Backgrounds are musical figures played to support a soloist.

1. Memorize the following riff patterns and use them as a basis for your own improvisations.

2. Alternate background riffs and improvisations. In each pattern, play the first two measures, and then substitute your own two-measure improvisation. Play measures 5–6 as written, then substitute your own improvisation for measures 7–8. Then do the set again, but start with your own improvised solo. Repeat the pattern.

3. Frame your improvisation. In each pattern, play the first part of the riff (measures 1–2), then substitute measures 3–6 with your own improvised solo, then play the last part of the riff (measures 7–8) as written. Repeat the pattern.

4. Improvise your own eight-measure riff patterns using the G pentatonic scale. Transcribe the recorded solos from the CD by writing them down or playing along with the recording.

Use the above procedures for improvising solos with the CD.

Background 1

Background 2

LESSON 2

THEORY

Jazz Staccato Quarter Notes

Jazz staccato quarter notes are played with a short, heavy attack. Quarter notes marked in this fashion (∧) are held for two-thirds of a beat. The sound "dot" best approximates how a jazz quarter note should be played.

Jazz Staccato Study

Lester Young Half Notes

Half notes marked thus (∧) are played with full intensity up to the count of two and then cut off. The sound "doot" best approximates how the longer cut-off note is to be played.

Lester Young Half-Notes Study

Mixed Articulation Study

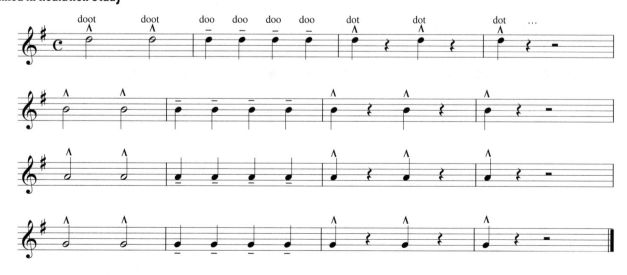

Workshop

Using combinations of notes derived from the G pentatonic scale, write and play at least two melodies using mixed articulations. Refer to the "Mixed Articulation Study" as your guide.

RHYTHM TRAINING

 Listen to CD Track 5.

1. **Echo.** Repeat each rhythm you hear exactly as it sounds on the recording.

2. **Answer.** Answer each rhythm you hear with your own improvised rhythm.

For the two-measure rhythm patterns below:

1. **Memorize.** Practice each pattern until you can play it without looking at the music.

2. **Compose.** Write at least four of your own rhythm patterns. Play and memorize these as well.

3. **Improvise/Transcribe.** Invent at least four of your own patterns by ear, memorize them, and then write them down.

Challenge

With another player, try the following:

1. **Reading call-and-response.** Player 1 plays one of the above rhythm patterns. Player 2 repeats it without looking at the music. Then switch roles.

2. **Improvising call-and-response.** Player 1 improvises a two-measure rhythm pattern. Player 2 repeats it. Then switch roles.

PERFORMANCE EAR TRAINING

 Listen to CD Track 6.

1. **Echo.** Repeat each motive you hear exactly as it sounds on the recording.

2. **Answer.** Answer each motive you hear with your own improvised motive. Your melodies should be derived from combinations of notes taken from the G pentatonic scale and the available blues notes. Try to use varied rhythms and combinations of articulation.

For the two-measure melodic motives below:

1. **Memorize.** Practice each motive until you can play it without looking at the music.

2. **Compose.** Write at least four of your own melodic motives. Play and memorize these as well.

3. **Improvise/Transcribe.** Invent at least four of your own motives by ear, memorize them, and then write them down.

Challenge

With another player, try the following:

1. **Reading call-and-response.** Player 1 plays one of the above motives. Player 2 repeats it without looking at the music. Then switch roles.

2. **Improvising call-and-response.** Player 1 improvises a two-measure motive. Player 2 repeats it. Then switch roles.

1. Learn the melody as written.

2. Play along with the recording. Try to capture the same manner of phrasing and style of playing.

   A Section. Head.
   - Melody for 16 measures (A1–A16)
   - You solo for 16 measures (A17–32). Use notes derived from the G pentatonic scale.

   B Section. Trading Eights.
   - Recorded solo for 8 measures

   C Section. Trading Eights.
   - You solo for 8 measures

   D Section. Trading Fours.
   - Recorded solo for 4 measures (D1–D4)
   - You solo for measures (D5–D8)
   - Recorded solo for 4 measures (D9–D12)
   - You solo for 4 measures (D13–16)

   E Section. Trading Twos.
   - Recorded solo for 2 measures (E1–E2)
   - You solo for 2 measures (E3–E4)
   - Recorded solo for 2 measures (E5–E6)
   - You solo for 2 measures (E7–E8)
   - Recorded solo for 2 measures (E9–E10)
   - You solo for 2 measures (E11–E12)
   - Recorded solo for 2 measures (E13–E14)
   - You solo for 2 measures (E15–E16)
   - At *D.S. al Coda*, return to sign at A.

   A Section (at repeat sign). Head.
   - Melody for 15 measures (A1–A15)
   - At sign, go to Coda.

   Coda.
   - Play 4X and fade.

L.Y.'s Domain

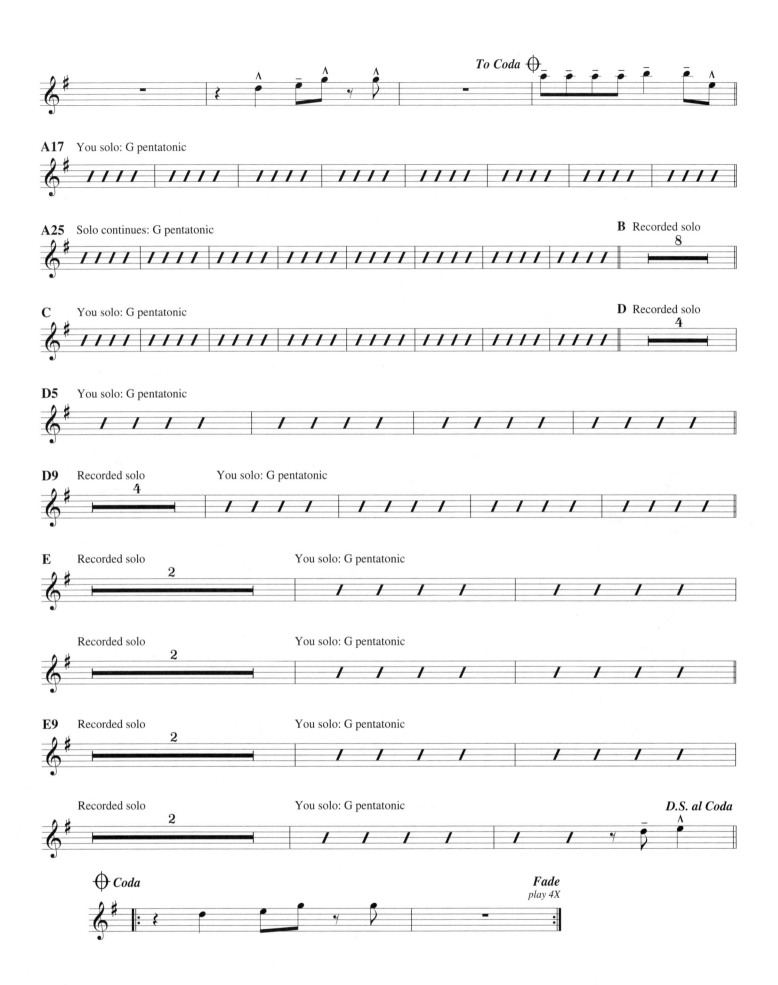

Backgrounds for "L.Y.'s Domain"

1. Memorize the following riff patterns and use them as a basis for your own improvisations.

2. Alternate background riffs and improvisations. In each pattern, play the first two measures, and then substitute your own two-measure improvisation. Play measures 5–6 as written, then substitute your own improvisation for measures 7–8. Then do the set again, but start with your own improvised solo. Repeat the pattern.

3. Frame your improvisation. In each pattern, play the first part of the riff (measures 1–2), then substitute measures 3–6 with your own improvised solo, then play the last part of the riff (measures 7–8) as written. Repeat the pattern.

4. Improvise your own eight-measure riff patterns using the G pentatonic scale. Transcribe the recorded solos from the CD by writing them down or playing along with the recording.

Use the above procedures for improvising solos with the CD.

12

LESSON 3

THEORY

G Pentatonic Scale

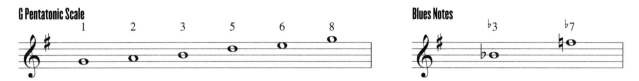

Blues Notes Study 1

Blues Notes Study 2

Workshop

Write and play at least two original eight-measure melodies. Use combinations of notes from the G pentatonic scale and available blues notes to create your melodies. Refer to the "Blues Notes Studies" as guides.

Evolving Rhythms

Play and write a two-measure rhythm pattern.

Use the following sounds to indicate the various jazz articulations.

        Connected notes (legato-staccato)

        Short notes (jazz staccato)

        Lester Young half notes

Note: Express these rhythms using any note from the G pentatonic scale.

Pattern A:

Pattern B: Start with the second measure of Pattern A and add a new rhythm.

Pattern C: Start with the second measure of Pattern B and add a new rhythm.

Pattern D: Start with the second measure of Pattern C and add a new rhythm.

Workshop

1. Use this study as a guide and create your own eight-measure evolving rhythm.

2. Play your own evolving rhythm, and make it swing.

RHYTHM TRAINING

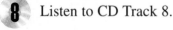 Listen to CD Track 8.

1. **Echo.** Repeat each rhythm you hear exactly as it sounds on the recording.

2. **Answer.** Answer each rhythm you hear with your own improvised rhythm.

For the two-measure rhythm patterns below:

1. **Memorize.** Practice each pattern until you can play it without looking at the music.

2. **Compose.** Write at least four of your own rhythm patterns. Play and memorize these as well.

3. **Improvise/Transcribe.** Invent at least four of your own rhythm patterns by ear, memorize them, and then write them down.

Challenge

With another player, try the following:

1. **Reading call-and-response.** Player 1 plays one of the above patterns. Player 2 repeats it without looking at the music. Then switch roles.

2. **Improvising call-and-response.** Player 1 improvises a two-measure pattern. Player 2 repeats it. Then switch roles.

Evolving Melodies

1. Write a melody to your eight-measure evolving rhythm. Use combinations of notes derived from the G pentatonic scale and the available blues notes.

2. Play your melody.

3. Improvise a new melody based on your eight-measure evolving rhythm.

PERFORMANCE EAR TRAINING

9 Listen to CD Track 9.

1. **Echo.** Repeat each motive you hear exactly as it sounds on the recording.

2. **Answer.** Answer each motive you hear with your own improvised motive. Your melodies should be derived from combinations of notes taken from the G pentatonic scale and the available blues notes. Try to use varied rhythms and combinations of articulation.

For the two-measure melodic motives below:

1. **Memorize.** Practice each motive until you can play it without looking at the music.

2. **Compose.** Write at least four of your own melodic motives. Play and memorize these as well.

3. **Improvise/Transcribe.** Invent at least four of your own motives by ear, memorize them, and then write them down.

Challenge

With another player, try the following:

1. **Reading call-and-response.** Player 1 plays one of the above motives. Player 2 repeats it without looking at the music. Then switch roles.

2. **Improvising call-and-response.** Player 1 improvises a two-measure motive. Player 2 repeats it. Then switch roles.

10 PERFORMANCE

1. Learn the melody as written.

2. Play along with the recording. Try to capture the same manner of phrasing and style of playing.

A Section. Head. Full ensemble.

- Melody for 12 measures

B Section. You solo.

- 24 measures (2 choruses). Use combinations of notes derived from the G pentatonic scale to create your solo.

C Section. Trading solos.

- Recorded solo for 12 measures (C1–C12)

- You solo for 4 measures (C13–C16)

- Recorded solo for 4 measures (C17–C20)

- You solo for 4 measures (C21–C24). At *D.S. al Coda*, return to the sign at letter A.

A Section (repeat). Head.

- Melody for 11 measures (A1–A11). At coda sign, go to Coda.

Coda.

- End held note with recording.

I'VE GOT THE BLUES

Backgrounds for "I've Got the Blues"

1. Memorize the following riff patterns and use them as a basis for your own improvisations.

2. Alternate background riffs and improvisations. In each pattern, play the first four measures, and then substitute your own four-measure improvisation. Play measures 9–10 as written, then substitute your own improvisation for measures 11–12. Then do the set again, but start with your own improvised solo. Repeat the pattern.

3. Frame your improvisation. In each pattern, play the first part of the riff (measures 1–4), then substitute measures 5–8 with your own improvised solo, then play the last part of the riff (measures 9–12) as written. Repeat the pattern.

4. Improvise your own eight-measure riff patterns using the G pentatonic scale. Transcribe the recorded solos from the CD by writing them down or playing along with the recording.

Workshop

1. Write a twelve-measure solo to be played at letter B along with the recording. Practice it alone until you can play it well. Play the solo along with the recording.

2. Transcribe the recorded solo either by writing it down or playing along with it.

Group Performance (without the CD)

Repeat B several times to extend your solo. Then repeat B several times for other players. Alternate four-measure solos through C. Take the *D.S.* and ending.

LESSON 4

THEORY

D Pentatonic Scale

Blues Notes

Smear

Attack each note below pitch and bring it up. This achieves the effect of saying, "doo-wah."

Note: Slide from the first note into the second note in the odd measures. Measures 2, 4, 6, and 8 are to be played in the same manner of each preceding measure.

Five Tone Study in D

Use of Blues Notes

Evolving Rhythms

Continue the practice outlined in Lesson 3 under Evolving Rhythms. Try to achieve as much variety as possible. Remember, it's important to make these rhythms swing and sound natural.

Evolving Melodies

1. Compose a four-measure melody based on the D blues scale using only half notes. Play your melody using legato-staccato articulations.

Phrase A

2. Change the last two measures of your original melody. Play this revised melody.

Phrase B

3. Change the first two measures of your first revision. Play this second revision.

Phrase C

4. Repeat steps (2) and (3) several times. Notice how your melody evolves.

RHYTHM TRAINING

 Listen to CD Track 11.

1. Echo. Repeat each rhythm you hear exactly as it sounds on the recording.

2. Answer. Answer each rhythm you hear with your own improvised rhythm.

For the two-measure rhythm patterns below:

1. Memorize. Practice each pattern until you can play it without looking at the music.

2. Compose. Write at least four of your own rhythm patterns. Play and memorize these as well.

3. Improvise/Transcribe. Invent at least four of your own patterns by ear, memorize them, and then write them down.

Challenge

With another player, try the following:

1. Reading call-and-response. Player 1 plays one of the above rhythm patterns. Player 2 repeats it without looking at the music. Then switch roles.

2. Improvising call-and-response. Player 1 improvises a two-measure rhythm pattern. Player 2 repeats it. Then switch roles.

PERFORMANCE EAR TRAINING

12 Listen to CD Track 12.

1. **Echo.** Repeat each motive you hear exactly as it sounds on the recording.

2. **Answer.** Answer each motive you hear with your own improvised motive. Your melodies should be derived from combinations of notes taken from the D pentatonic scale and the available blues notes. Try to use varied rhythms and combinations of articulation.

For the two-measure melodic motives below:

1. **Memorize.** Practice each motive until you can play it without looking at the music.

2. **Compose.** Write at least four of your own melodic motives. Play and memorize these as well.

3. **Improvise/Transcribe.** Invent at least four of your own motives by ear, memorize them, and then write them down.

Challenge

With another player, try the following:

1. **Reading call-and-response.** Player 1 plays one of the above motives. Player 2 repeats it without looking at the music. Then switch roles.

2. **Improvising call-and-response.** Player 1 improvises a two-measure motive. Player 2 repeats it. Then switch roles.

13 ▶ PERFORMANCE

1. Learn the melody as written.

2. Play along with the recording. Try to capture the same manner of phrasing and style of playing.

   Intro. Rhythm section.
   - 4 measures

   A Section. Head. Full ensemble.
   - Melody for 30 measures (1 chorus) (A1–A30)
   - Solo break (you) for 2 measures, leading into B section (A31–A32)

   B Section. You solo.
   - 32 measures (1 chorus) (B1–B32)

   C Section. Recorded solo.
   - 16 measures

   D Section. Trading Fours.
   - You solo for 4 measures (D1–D4)
   - Drum solo for 4 measures (D5–D8)
   - Recorded solo for 4 measures (D9–D12)
   - Drum solo for 4 measures (D13–D16)
   - You solo for for 4 measures (D17–D20)
   - Drum solo for 4 measures (D21–D24)
   - Recorded solo for 4 measures (D25–D28)
   - Drum solo for 4 measures (D29–D32)

   E Section. Head. Full ensemble.
   - Melody for 16 measures and finish

THE BRIGHTER SIDE

22

Workshop

1. Write a solo for B, D1 and D17 using combinations of tones derived form the D pentatonic scale and available blues notes. Practice it alone, then play it with the record.

2. Try to transcribe the recorded solo at letter B.

Backgrounds for "The Brighter Side"

1. Memorize the following riff patterns and use them as a basis for your own improvisations.

2. Alternate portions of riffs and improvisations. In each pattern, play the first two measures, then substitute your own two-measure improvisation. Play measures 5–6 as written, then substitute your own improvisation for measures 7–8. Then do the set again, but start with your own improvised solo. Repeat the pattern.

3. Frame your improvisation. In each pattern, play the first part of the riff (measures 1–2), then substitute measures 3–6 with your own improvised solo, then play the last part of the riff (measures 7–8) as written. Repeat the pattern.

4. Improvise your own eight-measure riff patterns using the D pentatonic scale.

5. Transcribe the recorded solos from the CD by writing them down or playing along with the recording.

6. Use the above procedures for improvising solos with the CD.

Background 1

Background 2

Background 3

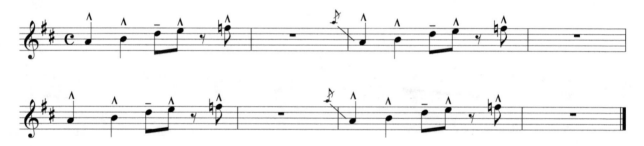

Group Performance (without the CD)

Repeat B for added choruses to your original solo. After you have completed your solo, continue repeating B for the other soloists in your group. When all the soloists have finished, skip C and proceed through the rest of the arrangement in this manner.

1. D1 You solo: first four measures

2. D5 Drum solo: second four measures

3. D9 Other soloist: third four measures

4. D13 Drum solo: fourth four measures

Continue playing from D to E several times, rotating soloists (trade fours) with the drummer. When finished, continue through letter E and conclude the arrangement.

LESSON 5

THEORY

Accents on Strong Beats

Connect notes as much as possible even though they are accented.

Accents on Weak Beats

Rhythm Displacement (Anticipation)

Anticipations can be used to create variety. They serve as a rhythmic contrast to regular rhythms.

1. Write and play a two-measure melody using half notes only.

   Example:

2. Write and play the same two-measure melody, but anticipate each attack by an eighth note.
   Example:

3. Write and play the same two-measure melody, but anticipate by a quarter note.
   Example:

4. Compose and play a melody using contrasting two-measure rhythms.
   Example:

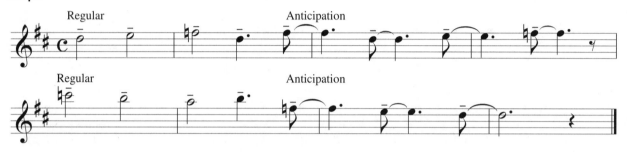

1. Write and play a two-measure melody using quarter notes only.
   Example:

2. Write and play the same two-measure melody, but anticipate each quarter note attack by an eighth note.
   Example:

3. Write and play a melody using contrasting two-measure rhythms.
   Example:

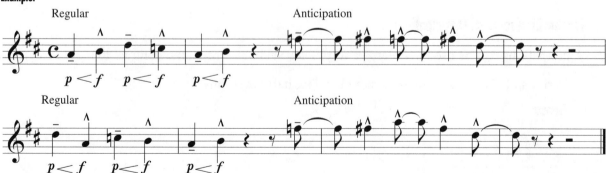

4. Use combinations of half notes and quarter notes. Combine with regular rhythms and anticipations.

Example:

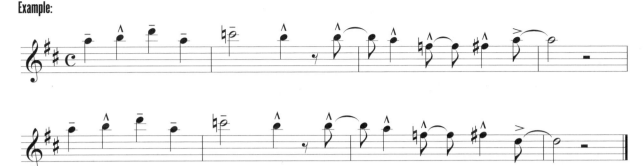

Workshop

1. **Anticipations.** Write, sing, and play your own eight-measure melody using combinations of regular rhythms and anticipations.

2. **Evolving Rhythm.** Write, sing, and play an eight-measure evolving rhythm melody that incorporates some anticipations.

3. **Evolving Melody.** Write, sing, and play an eight-measure evolving melody that incorporates some anticipations.

RHYTHM TRAINING

14 Listen to CD Track 14.

1. **Echo.** Repeat each rhythm you hear exactly as it sounds on the recording.

2. **Answer.** Answer each rhythm you hear with your own improvised rhythm.

For the two-measure rhythm patterns below:

1. **Memorize.** Practice each rhythm pattern until you can play it without looking at the music.

2. **Compose.** Write at least four of your own rhythm patterns. Play and memorize these as well.

3. **Improvise/Transcribe.** Invent at least four of your own rhythm patterns by ear, memorize them, and then write them down.

Challenge

With another player, try the following:

1. **Reading call-and-response.** Player 1 plays one of the above rhythm patterns. Player 2 repeats it without looking at the music. Then switch roles.

2. **Improvising call-and-response.** Player 1 improvises a two-measure rhythm pattern. Player 2 repeats it. Then switch roles.

PERFORMANCE EAR TRAINING

 Listen to CD Track 15.

1. **Echo.** Repeat each motive you hear exactly as it sounds on the recording.

2. **Answer.** Answer each motive you hear with your own improvised motive. Your melodies should be derived from combinations of notes taken from the D pentatonic scale and the available blues notes. Try to use varied rhythms and combinations of articulation.

For the two-measure melodic motives below:

1. **Memorize.** Practice each motive until you can play it without looking at the music.

2. **Compose.** Write at least four of your own melodic motives. Play and memorize these as well.

3. **Improvise/Transcribe.** Invent at least four of your own motives by ear, memorize them, and then write them down.

Challenge

With another player, try the following:

1. **Reading call-and-response.** Player 1 plays one of the above motives. Player 2 repeats it without looking at the music. Then switch roles.

2. **Improvising call-and-response.** Player 1 improvises a two-measure motive. Player 2 repeats it. Then switch roles.

16 PERFORMANCE

1. Learn the melody as written.

2. Play along with the recording. Try to capture the same manner of phrasing and style of playing.

   A Section. Head.

   - Melody for 32 measures

   B Section. You solo.

   - 32 measures (B1–B32). Use the D pentatonic scale and available blues notes.

   C Section. Trading solos.

   - Drum solo for 4 measures (C1–C4)

   - Recorded solo for 4 measures (C5–C9)

   - You solo for 8 measures (C9–C16)

   - Drum solo for 4 measures (C17–C20)

   - Recorded solo for 4 measures (C21–C24)

   - You solo for 8 measures (C25–C32)

   D Section. Head. Full ensemble.

   - Melody for 16 measures (D1–D16)

   - Final ending measure (D17)

WHERE'S PABLO?

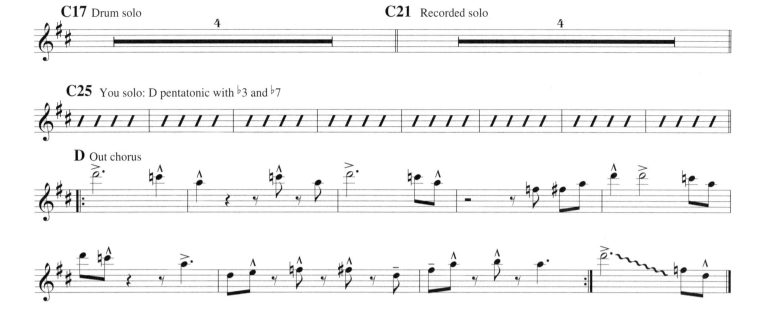

Backgrounds for "Where's Pablo?"

1. Memorize these riff patterns and use them as a basis for your own improvisations.

2. Alternate portions of riffs and improvisations. In each pattern, play the first two measures, then substitute your own two-measure improvisation. Play measures 5–6 as written, then substitute your own improvisation for measures 7–8. Then do the set again, but start with your own improvised solo. Repeat the pattern.

3. Frame your improvisation. In each pattern, play the first part of the riff (measures 1–2), then substitute measures 3–6 with your own improvised solo, then play the last part of the riff (measures 7–8) as written. Repeat the pattern.

4. Improvise your own eight-measure riff patterns using the D pentatonic scale.

Background 1

Background 2

31

Background 3

Workshop

1. Write a solo for measures B1–B8 and C9–C16. Use combinations of tones derived from the D pentatonic scale and the available blues notes. Practice it alone, then play it with the recording.

2. Transcribe the recorded solo at C5

3. Transcribe the rhythms played by the drums at C and C17.

Group Performance (without the CD)

Repeat letter B to letter C for added choruses to your original solo. After you have completed your solo, continue repeating B for the other soloists in your group. When all the soloists have finished, play through letter C in this manner:

1. C Drum solo: first four measures

2. C5 Other soloist: second four measures

3. C9 You solo: third four measures

4. C13 Drum solo: fourth four measures

Continue "trading fours" with the drummer until you are ready to continue through the rest of the arrangement. Play through letter D and conclude.

LESSON 6

THEORY

Accents Study 1

doo DOO   doo DOO   ...

Accents Study 2

Continue rhythmic interpretation the same manner as in the first measure.

Rhythm Displacement (Delayed Attack)

Delayed attacks can be used to create variety. They serve as a rhythmic contrast to regular rhythms.

1. Write and play a two-measure melody using half notes only.

   Example:

2. Write and play the same two-measure melody, but delay each note by an eighth note.

   Example:

3. Write and play the same two-measure melody, but delay each note by a quarter note.

   Example:

4. Compose and play a melody using contrasting two-measure rhythms.
   Example:

1. Write and play a two-measure melody using quarter notes only.
   Example:

2. Write and play the same two-measure melody, but delay each quarter note by an eighth note.
   Example:

3. Write and play a melody using contrasting two-measure rhythms.
   Example:

17 RHYTHM TRAINING

Listen to CD Track 17.

1. **Echo.** Repeat each rhythm you hear exactly as it sounds on the recording.

2. **Answer.** Answer each rhythm you hear with your own improvised rhythm.

For the two-measure rhythm patterns below:

1. **Memorize.** Practice each rhythm pattern until you can play it without looking at the music.

2. **Compose.** Write at least four of your own rhythm patterns. Play and memorize these as well.

3. **Improvise/Transcribe.** Invent at least four of your own rhythm patterns by ear, memorize them, and then write them down.

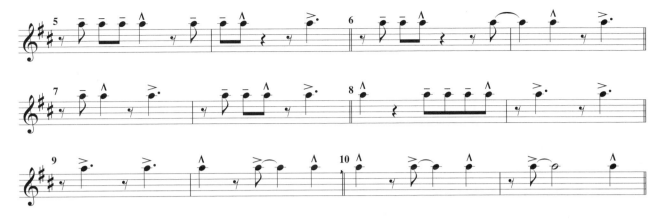

Challenge

With another player, try the following:

1. **Reading call-and-response.** Player 1 plays one of the above rhythm patterns. Player 2 repeats it without looking at the music. Then switch roles.

2. **Improvising call-and-response.** Player 1 improvises a two-measure rhythm pattern. Player 2 repeats it. Then switch roles.

PERFORMANCE EAR TRAINING

18 Listen to CD Track 18.

1. **Echo.** Repeat each motive you hear exactly as it sounds on the recording.

2. **Answer.** Answer each motive you hear with your own improvised motive. Your melodies should be derived from combinations of notes taken from the D pentatonic scale and the available blues notes. Try to use varied rhythms and combinations of articulation.

For the two-measure melodic motives below:

1. **Memorize.** Practice each motive until you can play it without looking at the music.

2. **Compose.** Write at least four of your own melodic motives. Play and memorize these as well.

3. **Improvise/Transcribe.** Invent at least four of your own motives by ear, memorize them, and then write them down.

Challenge

With another player, try the following:

1. **Reading call-and-response.** Player 1 plays one of the above motives. Player 2 repeats it without looking at the music. Then switch roles.

2. **Improvising call-and-response.** Player 1 improvises a two-measure motive. Player 2 repeats it. Then switch roles.

19 PERFORMANCE

A Section. Trading Twos and Fours.
- Recorded solo for 2 measures (A1–A2)
- You solo for 2 measures (A3–A4)

    [continue trading Twos until A17]
- Recorded solo for 4 measures (A17–A20)
- You solo for 4 measures (A21–A24)
- Recorded solo for 4 measures (A25–A28)
- Drum solo for 4 measures (A29–A32)

B Section. You solo.
- 32 measures

C Section. Trading Eights.
- Recorded solo for 8 measures (C1–C8)
- You solo for 8 measures (C9–C16)
- Bass solo for 8 measures (C17–C24)
- Drum solo for 8 measures (C25–C32)

D Section. Out Chorus.

1. Learn the melody as written.

2. Play along with the recording. Try to capture the same manner of phrasing and style of playing.
    - Cut off with the recording on the held last note.

CROSS FIRE

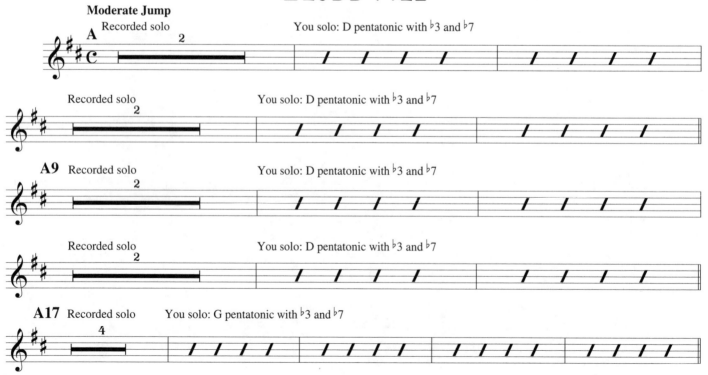

Backgrounds for "Cross Fire"

1. Memorize the following riff patterns and use them as a basis for your own improvisations.

2. Alternate portions of riffs and improvisations. In each pattern, play the first four measures, then substitute your own four-measure improvisation. Play measures 9–12 as written, then substitute your own improvisation for measures 13–16. Then do the set again, but start with your own improvised solo. Repeat the pattern.

3. Frame your improvisation. In each pattern, play the first part of the riff (measures 1–4), then substitute measures 5–12 with your own improvised solo, then play the last part of the riff (measures 13–16) as written. Repeat the pattern.

4. Improvise your own eight-measure riff patterns using the D pentatonic scale.

5. Transcribe the recorded solos from the CD by writing them down or playing along with the recording.

6. Use the above procedures for improvising solos with the CD.

Background 1

Background 3

Workshop

1. Write solos for measures A21–A24 and B1–B16.

2. Transcribe the recorded solos at A17 and C.

Group Performance (without the CD)

Trade two-measure solos from A1–A16. Then trade four-measure solos from A17–A28. Drum solo from A29–A32. Repeat letter B to letter C for added choruses to your original solo. After you have completed your solo, continue repeating letter B for the other soloists in your group. After all the soloists have finished, skip letter C and play the out chorus at letter D. Hold at the fermata ($\frown$) and cut off.

LESSON 7

THEORY

C Pentatonic Scale

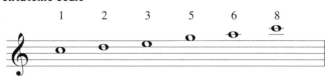

Blues Notes

C Pentatonic Scale

C Blues Study

Workshop

Write and play eight-measure melodies using the C pentatonic scale and available blues notes.

Combined Accents 1

Combined Accents 2

Workshop

Write and play eight-measure melodies using combined accents.

Rhythm Displacement

The use of anticipations, delayed attacks, and rests.

1. Write a two-measure melody using half notes.
   Example:

2. Write the same two-measure melody but use anticipations, delayed attacks, and rests to create rhythm displacement.
   Example:

3. Write an eight-measure melody using regular rhythms and rhythm displacement.
   Example:

1. Write a two-measure melody using quarter notes.
   Example:

2. Write the same two-measure melody but use anticipations, delayed attacks, and rests to create rhythm displacement.
   Example:

3. Write an eight-measure melody utilizing regular rhythms and rhythm displacement.
   Example:

Workshop

1. Write and play eight-measure melodies using combinations of regular rhythms and rhythm displacement.

2. Continue writing and playing eight-measure examples of evolving rhythms.

3. Continue writing and playing eight-measure examples of evolving melodies.

RHYTHM TRAINING

20 Listen to CD Track 20.

1. Echo. Repeat each rhythm you hear exactly as it sounds on the recording.

2. Answer. Answer each rhythm you hear with your own improvised rhythm.

For the two-measure rhythm patterns below:

1. Memorize. Practice each pattern until you can play it without looking at the music.

2. Compose. Write at least four of your own rhythm patterns. Play and memorize these as well.

3. Improvise/Transcribe. Invent at least four of your own rhythm patterns by ear, memorize them, and then write them down.

Challenge

With another player, try the following:

1. Reading call-and-response. Player 1 plays one of the above rhythm patterns. Player 2 repeats it without looking at the music. Then switch roles.

2. Improvising call-and-response. Player 1 improvises a two-measure rhythm pattern. Player 2 repeats it. Then switch roles.

PERFORMANCE EAR TRAINING

21 Listen to CD Track 21.

1. **Echo.** Repeat each motive you hear exactly as it sounds on the recording.

2. **Answer.** Answer each motive you hear with your own improvised motive. Your melodies should be derived from combinations of notes taken from the C pentatonic scale and available blues notes. Try to use varied rhythms and combinations of articulation.

For the two-measure melodic motives below:

1. **Memorize.** Practice each motive until you can play it without looking at the music.

2. **Compose.** Write at least four of your own melodic motives. Play and memorize these as well.

3. **Improvise/Transcribe.** Invent at least four of your own motives by ear, memorize them, and then write them down.

Challenge

With another player, try the following:

1. **Reading call-and-response.** Player 1 plays one of the above motives. Player 2 repeats it without looking at the music. Then switch roles.

2. **Improvising call-and-response.** Player 1 improvises a two-measure motive. Player 2 repeats it. Then switch roles.

1. Learn the melody as written.

2. Play along with the recording. Try to capture the same manner of phrasing and style of playing.

   A Section. Head. Full ensemble.

   - Melody for 16 measures

   B Section. You solo.

   - 16 measures. Use notes derived from the C pentatonic scale and available blues notes to create your melodies.

   X Interlude. Full ensemble.

   - 8 measures

   C Section. Trading Eights.

   - You solo for 8 measures (C1–C8). Use notes derived from the C pentatonic scale and available blues notes to make up your melodies.

   - Recorded solo for 8 measures (C9–16)

   D Section. You solo.

   - 8 measures (D1–D8). Use notes derived from the C pentatonic scale and available blues notes to make up your melodies.

   E Section. Trading Eights.

   - Recorded solo for 8 measures (E1–E8)

   - You solo for 8 measures (E9–E16). Use notes derived from the D pentatonic scale and available blues notes to make up your melodies.

   F Section. Out Chorus. Full ensemble.

LATE COMER

Group Performance (without the CD)

Open up from letter B to letter C for extended solos. Play X. Tacet C, C9, D, E, and E9.

Play out chorus (Letter F).

LESSON 8

THEORY

Melodic Extension

1. Write a melodic motive (idea) with two or three notes.

   Example:

2. Repeat the melodic idea but add one or two notes to it.

   Example:

3. Repeat the previous melodic example but add one or two notes to it.

   Example:

4. Repeat the previous melody. Continue adding notes until you have written an eight-measure melody.

   Example:

Workshop

Write and play eight-measure examples using melodic extension.

A general melodic tendency is that a leap in one direction is often followed by a step in the opposite direction.

   Example:

Example:

Workshop

Write and play eight-measure melodies. Use wider intervals than before. (An interval is the space between two notes: steps and leaps.)

Example:

Workshop

Write and play eight-measure melodies using the C pentatonic scale and available blues notes.

Varied Accents (sporadic)

Workshop

Write and play eight-measure melodies using varied accents.

Rhythmic Displacement

1. Write eight-measure melodies using half notes and quarter notes. Use combinations of notes from the C pentatonic scale and available blues notes to make up your melodies.

Example:

2. Rewrite the previous melody using displacement. Use combinations of anticipation, delayed attack, and rests.

Example:

Workshop

1. Continue writing and playing eight-measure examples of evolving rhythms.

2. Continue writing and playing eight-measure examples of evolving melodies.

RHYTHM TRAINING

23 Listen to CD Track 23.

1. **Echo.** Repeat each rhythm you hear exactly as it sounds on the recording.

2. **Answer.** Answer each rhythm you hear with your own improvised rhythm.

For the two-measure rhythm patterns below:

1. **Memorize.** Practice each rhythm pattern until you can play it without looking at the music.

2. **Compose.** Write at least four of your own rhythm patterns. Play and memorize these as well.

3. **Improvise/Transcribe.** Invent at least four of your own rhythm patterns by ear, memorize them, and then write them down.

Challenge

With another player, try the following:

1. **Reading call-and-response.** Player 1 plays one of the above rhythm patterns. Player 2 repeats it without looking at the music. Then switch roles.

2. **Improvising call-and-response.** Player 1 improvises a two-measure rhythm pattern. Player 2 repeats it. Then switch roles.

PERFORMANCE EAR TRAINING

 Listen to CD Track 24.

1. **Echo.** Repeat each motive you hear exactly as it sounds on the recording.

2. **Answer.** Answer each motive you hear with your own improvised motive. Your melodies should be derived from combinations of notes taken from the C pentatonic scale and available blues notes. Try to use varied rhythms and combinations of articulation.

For the two-measure melodic motives below:

1. **Memorize.** Practice each motive until you can play it without looking at the music.

2. **Compose.** Write at least four of your own melodic motives. Play and memorize these as well.

3. **Improvise/Transcribe.** Invent at least four of your own motives by ear, memorize them, and then write them down.

Challenge

With another player, try the following:

1. **Reading call-and-response.** Player 1 plays one of the above motives. Player 2 repeats it without looking at the music. Then switch roles.

2. **Improvising call-and-response.** Player 1 improvises a two-measure motive. Player 2 repeats it. Then switch roles.

25 **PERFORMANCE**

1. Learn the melody as written.

2. Play along with the recording. Try to capture the same manner of phrasing and style of playing.

   A Section. Head. Full ensemble.

   - 24 measures (2 choruses)

   B Section. You solo.

   - You solo

     • C pentatonic and blues notes (B1–B4)

     • D pentatonic and blues notes (B5–B8)

     • C pentatonic (B9)

     • D pentatonic (B10)

     • C pentatonic (B11)

     • D pentatonic (B12)

   - Backgrounds (B13-B24). Solo (you) continues.

   - You solo continues

     • C pentatonic and blues notes (B25–B28)

     • D pentatonic and blues notes (B29–B32)

     • C pentatonic (B33)

     • D pentatonic (B34)

     • C pentatonic (B35)

     • D pentatonic (B36)

   C Section. Trading Fours (and Twos).

   - Recorded solo for 4 measures (C1–C4)

   - You solo for 4 measures (C5–C8). Use notes derived from the D pentatonic scale and available blues notes to create your melodies.

   - Recorded solo for 2 measures (C9–C10)

   - Drum solo for 2 measures (C11–C12)

   D Section. Out Chorus. Full ensemble.

   - 12 measures

JUST WALKIN'

Group Performance (without the CD)

Open up from letter B to letter C for extended solos. Tacet C and continue through the rest of the arrangement.

LESSON 9

THEORY

Varied Melodic Extension

1. Write a two-measure melodic motive.

    Example A:

2. Start with the second measure of your motive and add a measure to it.

    Example B:

3. Continue the same procedure.

    Example C:

4. Continue the same procedure.

    Example D:

5. Write and play the four two-measure motives as an eight-measure melody.

    Example E:

6. Rewrite and play the four two-measure motives in this order: A, C, B, D.

    Example:

7. Rewrite and play the four two-measure motives in this order D, C, B, A.

Example:

The following is a list of available combinations. Try some of them to see how they work. Some will work better than others. This is a good way to become aware of the many possibilities for variation in melodic extension.

1. A, B, C, D	9. B, C, A, D	17. C, D, A, B
2. A, C, B, D	10. B, C, D, A	18. C, D, B, A
3. A, B, D, C	11. B, D, A, C	19. D, A, B, C
4. A, C, D, B	12. B, D, C, A	20. D, A, C, B
5. A, D, B, C	13. C, A, B, D	21. D, B, A, C
6. A, D, C, B	14. C, A, D, B	22. D, B, C, A
7. B, A, D, C	15. C, B, A, D	23. D, C, A, B
8. B, A, C, D	16. C, B, D, A	24. D, C, B, A

Workshop

1. Write and play eight-measure examples using varied melodic extension.

2. Change these eight-measure examples, selecting from the list of available combinations as illustrated.

3. Continue writing and playing melodies using rhythm displacement.

4. Continue writing and playing eight-measure examples of evolving rhythms.

RHYTHM TRAINING

26 Listen to CD Track 26.

1. Echo. Repeat each rhythm you hear exactly as it sounds on the recording.

2. Answer. Answer each rhythm you hear with your own improvised rhythm.

For the two-measure rhythm patterns below:

1. Memorize. Practice each rhythm pattern until you can play it without looking at the music.

2. Compose. Write at least four of your own rhythm patterns. Play and memorize these as well.

3. Improvise/Transcribe. Invent at least four of your own rhythm patterns by ear, memorize them, and then write them down.

Challenge

With another player, try the following:

1. **Reading call-and-response.** Player 1 plays one of the above rhythm patterns. Player 2 repeats it without looking at the music. Then switch roles.

2. **Improvising call-and-response.** Player 1 improvises a two-measure rhythm pattern. Player 2 repeats it. Then switch roles.

PERFORMANCE EAR TRAINING

27 Listen to CD Track 27.

1. **Echo.** Repeat each motive you hear exactly as it sounds on the recording.

2. **Answer.** Answer each motive you hear with your own improvised motive. Your melodies should be derived from combinations of notes taken from the C pentatonic scale and available blues notes. Try to use varied rhythms and combinations of articulation.

For the two-measure melodic motives below:

1. **Memorize.** Practice each motive until you can play it without looking at the music.

2. **Compose.** Write at least four of your own melodic motives. Play and memorize these as well.

3. **Improvise/Transcribe.** Invent at least four of your own motives by ear, memorize them, and then write them down.

Challenge

With another player, try the following:

1. **Reading call-and-response.** Player 1 plays one of the above motives. Player 2 repeats it without looking at the music. Then switch roles.

2. **Improvising call-and-response.** Player 1 improvises a two-measure motive. Player 2 repeats it. Then switch roles.

28 PERFORMANCE

1. Learn the melody as written.

2. Play along with the recording. Try to capture the same manner of phrasing and style of playing.

   A Section. Head. Full ensemble.

   - Melody for 22 measures (A1–A22)
   - Solo break (you) continuing into B section (A23–24)

   B Section. You solo.

   - 48 measures (2 choruses)
   - C pentatonic with available blues notes (B1–B8)
   - G pentatonic with available blues notes (B9–B16)
   - C pentatonic with available blues notes (B17–B24)

   C Section. Solo (you) continues.

   - 24 measures
   - C pentatonic with available blues notes (C1–C8)
   - G pentatonic with available blues notes (C9–C16)
   - C pentatonic with available blues notes (C17–C24)

   D Section. Out Chorus.

   - Melody for 8 measures (D1–D8)
   - Trading Fours
     • You solo for 4 measures on G pentatonic with available blues notes (D9–D12)
     • Drum solo for 4 measures (D13–D16)
   - Melody for 8 measures (D17–D24)
   - Cut off with the recording on the held last note.

Playmates

D Out Chorus

D9 Solo (you) continues: G pentatonic with ♭3 and ♭7   Drum solo

D17

Fine

Backgrounds for "Playmates"

The following backgrounds are guide-tone lines. Guide-tone lines outline the harmonic movement of a song. Play the following guide-tone lines along with the CD at letter B. Listen to the bass line while playing along. Notice how the guide-tone lines reinforce the harmonic progression.

Guide-Tone Background 1

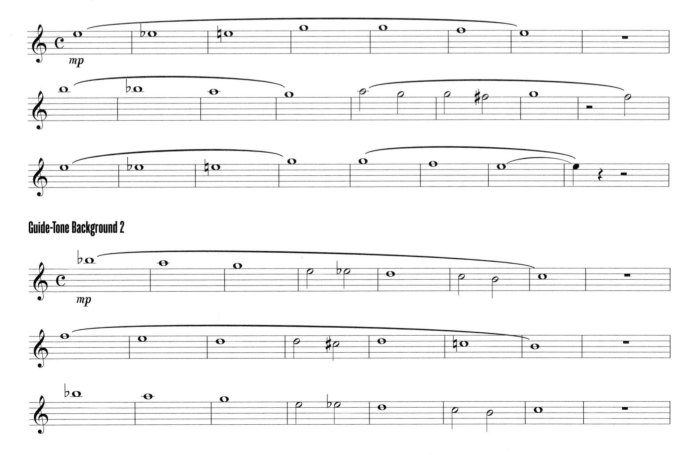

Guide-Tone Background 2

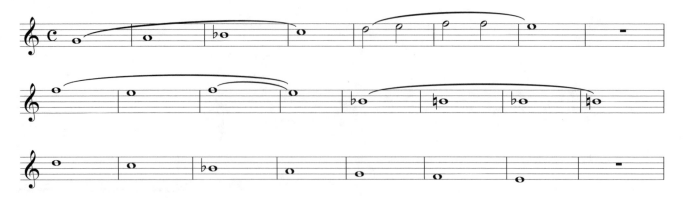

Workshop

Write a melodic improvisation for measures B1–B24. Practice it. Then try it with the recording at the place designated for your solo.

LESSON 10

THEORY

Combining Two Scale Centers in Eight-Measure Intervals

Write and play eight-measure melodies using different pentatonic scale centers.

1. Put the first four measures in G pentatonic.

Example:

2. Put the second four measures in C pentatonic. (Keep the G key signature.)

Example:

3. Combine (1) and (2).

Example:

4. Reverse procedure; write (2) then (1).

Example:

Note: The tune's key signature can be either G (one sharp) or C. The deciding factor would generally be the scale center of the tune's final measure.

The following is a list of possible combinations of pentatonic scale centers using scales we have covered so far.

	a. four measures	*b. four measures*
Combination 1.	G pentatonic	C pentatonic
Combination 2.	C pentatonic	G pentatonic
Combination 3.	G pentatonic	D pentatonic
Combination 4.	D pentatonic	G pentatonic
Combination 5.	C pentatonic	D pentatonic
Combination 6.	D pentatonic	C pentatonic

Workshop

Write and play eight-measure melodies made up of combinations of pentatonic scale centers. First work with Combination 1 above, then duplicate the procedure throughout the other combinations. Do as much of this as possible. It will prove helpful later in playing on standard songs.

Combining Two Scale Centers in Two-Measure Intervals

Write and play two-measure melodies using different pentatonic scale centers.

1. Write and play a two-measure motive using the G pentatonic scale and available blues notes.
   Example:

2. Write and play a two-measure motive using the C pentatonic scale and available blues notes.
   Example:

3. Combine (1) and (2).
   Example:

4. Add measures 5–6 by creating the melody from the G pentatonic scale and available blues notes.
   Example:

5. Add measures 7–8 by making up the melody from the C pentatonic scale and available blues notes.
   Example:

The following is a list of possible two-measure combinations of pentatonic scale centers using the scales that we have covered so far.

Measures 1–2	Measures 3–4	Measures 5–6	Measures 7–8
1. G pentatonic	C pentatonic	G pentatonic	C pentatonic
2. C pentatonic	G pentatonic	C pentatonic	C pentatonic
3. G pentatonic	————————▶	C pentatonic	G pentatonic
4. G pentatonic	C pentatonic	————————▶	G pentatonic
5. C pentatonic	————————▶	G pentatonic	C pentatonic
6. C pentatonic	G pentatonic	————————▶	C pentatonic
7. G pentatonic	D pentatonic	G pentatonic	G pentatonic
8. D pentatonic	G pentatonic	D pentatonic	G pentatonic
9. G pentatonic	————————▶	D pentatonic	G pentatonic
10. G pentatonic	D pentatonic	————————▶	G pentatonic
11. D pentatonic	————————▶	G pentatonic	D pentatonic
12. D pentatonic	G pentatonic	————————▶	D pentatonic
13. D pentatonic	C pentatonic	D pentatonic	C pentatonic
14. C pentatonic	D pentatonic	C pentatonic	D pentatonic
15. D pentatonic	————————▶	C pentatonic	D pentatonic
16. D pentatonic	C pentatonic	————————▶	D pentatonic
17. C pentatonic	————————▶	D pentatonic	C pentatonic
18. G pentatonic	D pentatonic	————————▶	C pentatonic

Workshop

1. Write and play melodies made up of the above combinations.

2. Continue writing and playing melodies as before using varied melodic extension, rhythm displacement, and evolving rhythms.

RHYTHM TRAINING

29 Listen to CD Track 29.

1. Echo. Repeat each rhythm you hear exactly as it sounds on the recording.

2. Answer. Answer each rhythm you hear with your own improvised rhythm.

For the two-measure rhythm patterns below:

1. **Memorize.** Practice each rhythm pattern until you can play it without looking at the music.

2. **Compose.** Write at least four of your own rhythm patterns. Play and memorize these as well.

3. **Improvise/Transcribe.** Invent at least four of your own rhythm patterns by ear, memorize them, and then write them down.

Challenge

With another player, try the following:

1. **Reading call-and-response.** Player 1 plays one of the above rhythm patterns. Player 2 repeats it without looking at the music. Then switch roles.

2. **Improvising call-and-response.** Player 1 improvises a two-measure rhythm pattern. Player 2 repeats it. Then switch roles.

PERFORMANCE EAR TRAINING

30 Listen to CD Track 30.

1. **Echo.** Repeat each motive you hear exactly as it sounds on the recording.

2. **Answer.** Answer each motive you hear with your own improvised motive. Try to use varied rhythms and combinations of articulation.

For the two-measure melodic motives below:

1. **Memorize.** Practice each motive until you can play it without looking at the music.

2. **Compose.** Write at least four of your own melodic motives. Play and memorize these as well.

3. **Improvise/Transcribe.** Invent at least four of your own motives by ear, memorize them, and then write them down.

Challenge

With another player, try the following:

1. **Reading call-and-response.** Player 1 plays one of the above motives. Player 2 repeats it without looking at the music. Then switch roles.

2. **Improvising call-and-response.** Player 1 improvises a two-measure motive. Player 2 repeats it. Then switch roles.

31 PERFORMANCE

1. Learn the melody as written.

2. Play along with the recording. Try to capture the same manner of phrasing and style of playing.

   A Section. Head.

   - Melody for 24 measures (2 choruses)

   B Section. You solo.

   - 24 measures (2 choruses)

   - G pentatonic and available blues notes (B1–B4)

   - C pentatonic and available blues notes (B5–B6)

   - G pentatonic and available blues notes (B7–B8)

   - D pentatonic and available blues notes (B9–B10)

   - G pentatonic and available blues notes (B11–B12)

   C Section. Out Chorus.

   - Play with the CD and finish.

The Blues Guide

Guide-Tone Melody 1

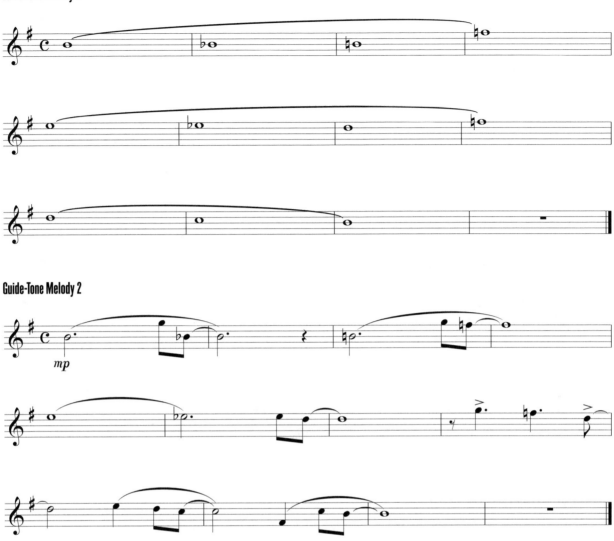

Guide-Tone Melody 2

Group Performance (without the CD)

By repeating the section from letter B to letter C any number of times, you can play more extended solos. After everyone has finished improvising their extended solos, you can alternate four-measure solos with the drummer. When you have finished playing alternate four-measure solos, proceed through letter C and finish playing the arrangement.

LESSON 11

THEORY

A Pentatonic Scale

Blues Notes

Exercise

Workshop

1. Practice Exercise 1 until you can play without stopping.

2. Write and play original melodic exercises based on the same scale.

Blues Guide Line

The guide line is made up of a series of connected whole notes and/or half notes. Its purpose is to give you a sense of direction and a musical reference point throughout the song. It can be learned quite easily. Memorize it and use it as a point of departure when creating your melodies.

Melodic Use of Blues Guide Line

Create melodies using the guide line as the core of your ideas. You can move away from the guide line either up or down.

You can approach the guide-tone line from above or below.

Blues Guide-Tone Line

Example:

Workshop

1. Play the top line of the Blues Guide-Tone Line until you have it memorized.

2. Play the bottom line and listen for the connecting guide tones.

3. Write and play your own twelve-measure melodies. Use guide tones, relevant pentatonic scales, and available blues notes in creating your melodies.

Combining Three Scale Centers

1. Write and play a four-measure melody using notes derived from the G pentatonic scale and available blues notes.

   Example:

2. Write and play a four-measure melody using notes derived from the C pentatonic scale and available blues notes.

   Example:

3. Combine (1) and (2).

   Example:

67

4. Write and play a four-measure melody using notes derived from the D pentatonic scale and available blues notes.

Example:

5. Combine 1, 2, and 4.

Example:

G pentatonic

C pentatonic

D pentatonic

Workshop

Write and play an original twelve-measure melody consisting of three four-measure phrases using scale centers as illustrated above.

The following is a list of possible three-scale-center combinations (four measures each) using scales we have covered so far.

Measures 1–4	Measures 5–8	Measures 9–12
1. G pentatonic	C pentatonic	D pentatonic
2. G pentatonic	D pentatonic	C pentatonic
3. G pentatonic	A pentatonic	D pentatonic
4. G pentatonic	D pentatonic	A pentatonic
5. G pentatonic	C pentatonic	A pentatonic
6. G pentatonic	A pentatonic	C pentatonic
7. C pentatonic	G pentatonic	D pentatonic
8. C pentatonic	G pentatonic	A pentatonic
9. C pentatonic	D pentatonic	G pentatonic
10. C pentatonic	D pentatonic	A pentatonic
11. C pentatonic	A pentatonic	D pentatonic
12. C pentatonic	A pentatonic	G pentatonic
13. D pentatonic	G pentatonic	A pentatonic
14. D pentatonic	A pentatonic	G pentatonic
15. D pentatonic	G pentatonic	C pentatonic
16. D pentatonic	C pentatonic	G pentatonic
17. D pentatonic	C pentatonic	A pentatonic

18. D pentatonic	A pentatonic	C pentatonic
19. A pentatonic	D pentatonic	G pentatonic
20. A pentatonic	G pentatonic	D pentatonic
21. A pentatonic	C pentatonic	G pentatonic
22. A pentatonic	G pentatonic	C pentatonic
23. A pentatonic	D pentatonic	C pentatonic
24. A pentatonic	C pentatonic	D pentatonic

RHYTHM TRAINING

32 Listen to CD Track 32.

1. Echo. Repeat each rhythm you hear exactly as it sounds on the recording.

2. Answer. Answer each rhythm you hear with your own improvised rhythm.

For the two-measure rhythm patterns below:

1. Memorize. Practice each rhythm pattern until you can play it without looking at the music.

2. Compose. Write at least four of your own rhythm patterns. Play and memorize these as well.

3. Improvise/Transcribe. Invent at least four of your own rhythm patterns by ear, memorize them, and then write them down.

Challenge

With another player, try the following:

1. Reading call-and-response. Player 1 plays one of the above rhythm patterns. Player 2 repeats it without looking at the music. Then switch roles.

2. Improvising call-and-response. Player 1 improvises a two-measure rhythm pattern. Player 2 repeats it. Then switch roles.

PERFORMANCE EAR TRAINING

33 Listen to CD Track 33.

1. **Echo.** Repeat each motive you hear exactly as it sounds on the recording.

2. **Answer.** Answer each motive you hear with your own improvised motive. Try to use varied rhythms and combinations of articulation.

For the two-measure melodic motives below:

1. **Memorize.** Practice each motive until you can play it without looking at the music.

2. **Compose.** Write at least four of your own melodic motives. Play and memorize these as well.

3. **Improvise/Transcribe.** Invent at least four of your own motives by ear, memorize them, and then write them down.

Challenge

With another player, try the following:

1. **Reading call-and-response.** Player 1 plays one of the above motives. Player 2 repeats it without looking at the music. Then switch roles.

2. **Improvising call-and-response.** Player 1 improvises a two-measure motive. Player 2 repeats it. Then switch roles.

34 PERFORMANCE

1. Learn the melody as written.

2. Play along with the recording. Try to capture the same manner of phrasing and style of playing.

   A Section. Head. Full ensemble.

   - Melody for 22 measures (A1–A22)

   - Solo break (you) continuing into B section (A23–24). Use notes derived from the D pentatonic scale and available blues notes.

   B Section. You solo.

   - 36 measures (3 choruses)

     Repeat this progression for each chorus:

     • D pentatonic and available blues notes (B1–B4)

     • G pentatonic with available blues notes (B5–B6)

     • D pentatonic with available blues notes (B7–B8)

     • A pentatonic with available blues notes (B9–B10)

     • D pentatonic with available blues notes (B11–B12)

   C Section. Trading Fours.

   - Recorded solo for 4 measures (C1–C4)

   - You solo for 4 measures (C5–C8)

   - Drum solo for 4 measures (C9–C12)

   D Section. Out Chorus.

   - Melody for 24 measures and finish

G.L. BLUES

Workshop

1. Write melodic solos for section B and measures C5–C8.

2. Practice these solos until you can play them comfortably.

3. Play these solos with the recording.

4. Transcribe the recorded solos.

Backgrounds

The following backgrounds are guide tone lines. Guide tone lines outline the harmonic movement of a song. Play the Blues Guide Line (2) along with the CD from B1–B12. Listen to the bass line while playing along. Notice how the guide tone lines reinforce the harmonic progression.

Backgrounds for "G.L. Blues"

Play the following backgrounds with the recording in the B section and use them as a basis for making up your own backgrounds.

Background 1

Background 2

Background 3

Group Performance (without the CD)

By repeating section B you can play more extended solos. After playing the extended solos, section C can be repeated for alternating four-measure solos. After completing the alternating four-measure solos, play the out chorus and finish.

LESSON 12

THEORY

Mixolydian Scale (Mode)

When scale centers change rapidly, it becomes difficult to change with them and necessary to find a more simple method of playing through them.

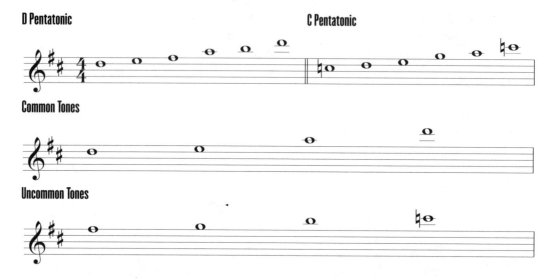

D Pentatonic **C Pentatonic**

Common Tones

Uncommon Tones

By combining the common and uncommon tones, it is possible to make up a scale that will function through both pentatonic scale centers. This scale is called the D Mixolydian scale or mode.

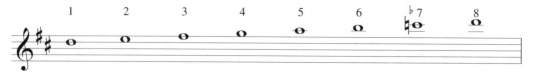

D Mixolydian Study

This scale can be used through D and C scale centers.

Workshop

1. Play "D Mixolydian Study."

2. Write and play original eight-measure melodies using the D Mixolydian scale.

A Mixolydian Scale

This scale can be used through G and A pentatonic scale centers.

A Mixolydian Study

Workshop

1. Play "A Mixolydian Study."

2. Write and play original eight-measure melodies using the A Mixolydian scale.

Calypso Guide Line 1

Example: Guide Line

Calypso Guide Line 2

Workshop

Create melodies using the guide line as the center of your ideas. Use melodic ideas as shown in the Melodic Use of Blues Guide Line, Lesson 11.

Example: Guide Line

RHYTHM TRAINING

35 Listen to CD Track 35.

1. **Echo.** Repeat each rhythm you hear exactly as it sounds on the recording.

2. **Answer.** Answer each rhythm you hear with your own improvised rhythm.

For the two-measure rhythm patterns below:

1. **Memorize.** Practice each rhythm pattern until you can play it without looking at the music.

2. **Compose.** Write at least four of your own rhythm patterns. Play and memorize these as well.

3. **Improvise/Transcribe.** Invent at least four of your own rhythm patterns by ear, memorize them, and then write them down.

Challenge

With another player, try the following:

1. **Reading call-and-response.** Player 1 plays one of the above rhythm patterns. Player 2 repeats it without looking at the music. Then switch roles.

2. **Improvising call-and-response.** Player 1 improvises a two-measure rhythm pattern. Player 2 repeats it. Then switch roles.

PERFORMANCE EAR TRAINING

36 Listen to CD Track 36.

1. **Echo.** Repeat each motive you hear exactly as it sounds on the recording.

2. **Answer.** Answer each motive you hear with your own improvised motive. Try to use varied rhythms and combinations of articulation.

For the two-measure melodic motives below:

1. **Memorize.** Practice each motive until you can play it without looking at the music.

2. **Compose.** Write at least four of your own melodic motives. Play and memorize these as well.

3. **Improvise/Transcribe.** Invent at least four of your own motives by ear, memorize them, and then write them down.

Challenge

With another player, try the following:

1. **Reading call-and-response.** Player 1 plays one of the above motives. Player 2 repeats it without looking at the music. Then switch roles.

2. **Improvising call-and-response.** Player 1 improvises a two-measure motive. Player 2 repeats it. Then switch roles.

37 PERFORMANCE

1. Learn the melody as written.

2. Play along with the recording. Try to capture the same manner of phrasing and style of playing.

   Intro. Drum solo

   - 4 measures

   A Section. Head.

   - Melody for 31 measures (A32)

   - You solo break (A32) continuing into B section. Use notes derived from the A Mixolydian scale.

   B Section. You solo.

   - 96 measures (3 choruses)

   - Use notes derived from the A Mixolydian scale.

   C Section. Drum solo.

   - 4 measures

   D Section. Out Chorus.

   - Melody for 16 measures and finish

WEST INDIA WAY

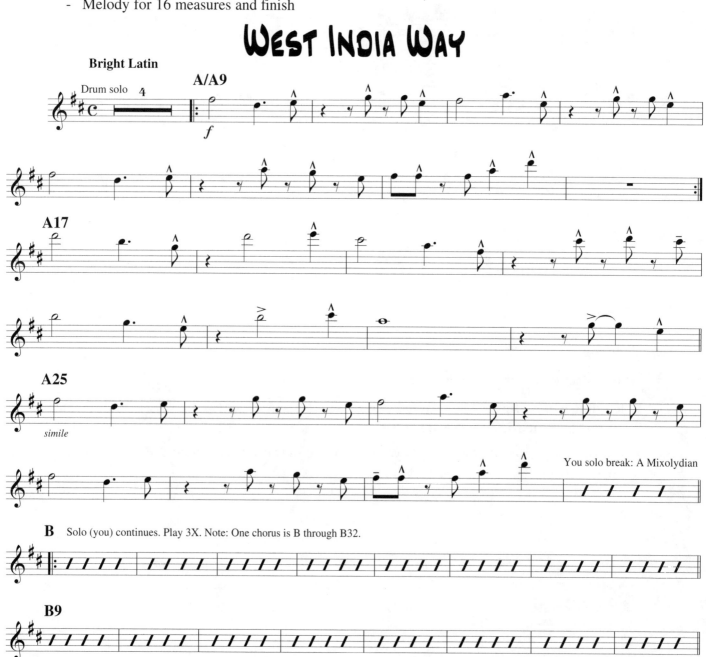

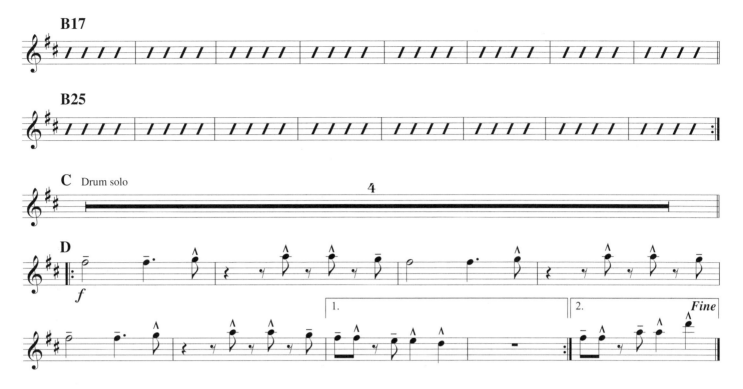

Workshop

1. Write melodic solos for section B.

2. Practice these solos until you can play them comfortably.

3. Play these solos with the recording.

4. Transcribe the recorded drum solo.

Backgrounds for "West India Way"

Background 1

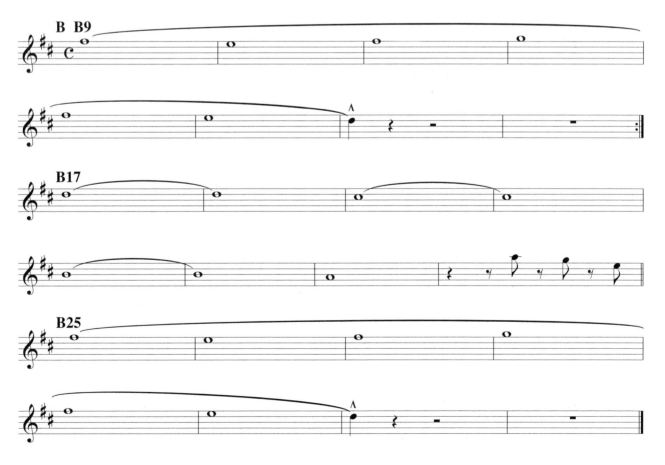

Background 2

Background 3

Group Performance (without the CD)

Continue repeating letter B to letter C for extended solos. When you have completed your solos, continue to play through the rest of the arrangement.

JOHN LAPORTA

John LaPorta has composed, arranged, performed, and recorded with Woody Herman, Herb Pomeroy, Kenny Clarke, and many others. He has recorded with Charlie Parker, Lester Young, Charles Mingus, Miles Davis, Dizzie Gillespie, Max Roach, Oscar Pettiford, Lennie Tristano, Buddy Rich, and Fats Navarro.

John has performed with the New York Philharmonic Symphony Orchestra under the direction of Leonard Bernstein, and was the soloist for the Everest Recording of Igor Stravinsky's "Ebony Concerto."

He taught for 37 years at Berklee College of Music and 25 years at National Stage Band Camps, and holds the title, Professor Emeritus, Berklee College of Music.

The International Association of Jazz Educators honored John LaPorta with the Humanitarian Award at its 1994 Annual Conference in Boston, MA. He has composed numerous works for high school stage bands, and several other educational texts.

After teaching jazz improvisation for more than fifty years, in 1999, John LaPorta retired to Sarasota, FL, with his wife, Virginia.

berklee press

Visit www.berkleepress.com

These books feature material developed at Berklee College of Music

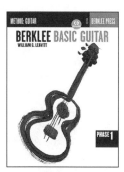

GUITAR PUBLICATIONS – *continued*

Rock Guitar Styles
by Mike Ihde

This popular hands-on book teaches modern guitarists how to play lead and rhythm guitar. Styles include heavy metal, hard rock, new wave, blues, jazz-rock, funk, and more. Many music examples and a demonstration cassette make this the player's method of choice. 33-minute audio accompaniment.

50449520 Book/Cassette Pack $14.95

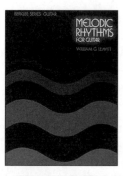

Melodic Rhythms for Guitar
by William Leavitt

A thorough presentation of rhythms commonly found in contemporary music, including 68 harmonized melodies and 42 rhythm exercises. The cassette features demonstration duets, as well as recorded rhythm-section accompaniments so that the student can play along.

50449450 Book..$14.95
50449452 Book/Cassette Pack...............................$16.95

Classical Studies for Pick-Style Guitar
by William Leavitt

An outstanding collection of solos and duets for intermediate to advanced pick-style guitarists. Includes 21 pieces by Carcassi, Carulli, Sor, Bach, Paganini, Kreutzer, and Clementi.

50449440 Book..$9.95

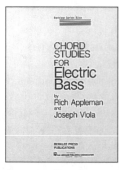

Chord Studies for Electric Bass
by Rich Appleman/Joseph Viola

This 162-page method thoroughly covers basic and extended chords in all keys. Melodic studies designed for the intermediate and advanced player develop all aspects of technique. Special emphasis is placed on playing in the higher register. This method can also be effectively used for acoustic bass study.

50449750 Book..$12.95

Prices and availability subject to change without notice.

BUSINESS GUIDES

The Self-Promoting Musician
by Peter Spellman

From the Director of Career Development at Berklee College of Music, learn how to become a success in the music business. Complete with tips for writing business plans and press kits; business know-how; using the Internet to promote music; customizing demos for maximum exposure; getting music played on college radio; and a comprehensive musician's resource list.

50449423 Book..$24.95

Complete Guide to Film Scoring
by Richard Davis

Learn the art and business of film scoring, including: the film-making process; preparing and recording a score; contracts and fees; publishing, royalties, and copyrights. Features interviews with 19 film-scoring professionals.

50449417 Book..$24.95

The New Music Therapist's Handbook – 2nd Edition
by Suzanne B. Hanser

Dr. Hanser's well respected *Music Therapist's Handbook* has been thoroughly updated and revised to reflect the latest developments in the field of music therapy. Includes: an introduction to music therapy; new clinical applications and techniques, case studies; designing, implementing, and evaluating individualized treatment programs, including guidelines for beginning music therapists.

50449424 Book..$29.95

Masters of Music Conversations with Berklee Greats
by Mark Small and Andrew Taylor

An impressive collection of personal interviews with music industry superstars from *Berklee Today*, the alumni magazine of Berklee College of Music. Read about how these luminaries got their breaks, and valuable lessons learned along the way. Paula Cole talks about navigating through the recording industry, George Martin on technology's effect on artistic freedom, Patty Larkin considers the creative process, and Alf Clausen discusses scoring *The Simpsons*. Get the story from these stars and many others.

50449422 Book..$24.95